Rh

My aim has been to ma_____ _____ ____
wide collection of vers_____ ___ ____ ____
were chosen for the st_____ __ _____,
helping children to b___ __ ____ of imaginative
experience. Others were chosen for their strong
verbal and rhythmic patterns, to show the young
child how words can be fun as well as a means of
communication. Walter de la Mare, Ian Serraillier,
James Reeves, Eleanor Farjeon, John Walsh and
Spike Milligan are a few of the well-known poets
represented, but there are also plenty of works by
young poets who may not yet be generally known,
and all have contributed rhymes that children will
want to hear over and over again.

B.I.

Also in Red Fox (incorporating Beaver Books)
by Barbara Ireson

Rhyme Time

poems collected by Barbara Ireson

Illustrated by Lesley Smith

RED FOX

A Red Fox Book

Published by Arrow Books Limited
20 Vauxhall Bridge Road, London SW1V 2SA

An imprint of the Random Century Group

London Melbourne Sydney Auckland
Johannesburg and agencies throughout
the world

First published 1977
Seventh impression 1990
Red Fox edition 1990
This collection © Barbara Ireson 1977
Illustrations © Century Hutchinson Ltd 1977

Printed and bound in Great Britain
by Cox & Wyman Ltd, Reading

ISBN 0 09 949650 X

Contents

Acknowledgements

The author and publishers would like to thank the following people for giving permission to include in this anthology material which is their copyright. The publishers have made every effort to trace copyright holders. If we have inadvertently omitted to acknowledge anyone we should be most grateful if this could be brought to our attention for correction at the first opportunity.

George Allen & Unwin (Publishers) Ltd for an extract from 'Errantry', and for 'Oliphaunt', both from *The Adventures of Tom Bombadil* by J. R. R. Tolkien

Angus & Robertson (U.K.) Ltd for 'Walter Spaggot', 'Skinny Winny' and 'The Ugstabuggle' from *The Ombley-Gombley* by Peter Wesley-Smith

Atheneum Publishers for 'Wind Song', 'Go Wind', 'Waking' and 'Dragon Smoke' from *I Feel the Same Way* by Lilian Moore (text copyright © 1967 by Lilian Moore); 'Squirrel', 'Green', 'Weather Report' and 'Wet' from *Sam's Place* by Lilian Moore (text copyright © 1973 by Lilian Moore)

Adam and Charles Black Publishers for 'Ducky-Daddles' from *Speech Rhymes* by Winifred Kingdon-Ward; 'Creeping' by Hilda Adams from *Rhythm Rhymes*

Basil Blackwell Publisher for 'Last Song' by James Guthrie; 'The Hare', 'Have You Ever ...?' 'Here Comes a Knight' and 'Jonathan' from *Widdy-Widdy-Wurky* by Rose Fyleman

Jonathan Cape Ltd, Holt Rinehart and Winston, Publishers and The Estate of Robert Frost for 'The Last Word of a Bluebird' from *The Poetry of Robert Frost*, edited by Edward Connery Lathem (copyright 1916, © 1969 by Holt, Rinehart and Winston, copyright 1944 by Robert Frost)

Chatto & Windus for 'The Old Field' from *Rhyme Times Rhyme* by D. J. Enright; 'Dead Blackbird' from *A Song of Sunlight* by Phoebe Hesketh

William Cole for 'Oh, Who Will Wash the Tiger's Ears?' by Shel Silverstein (copyright © 1967 Shel Silverstein)

Curtis Brown Ltd, London on behalf of the Estate of A. A. Milne for 'The Young Puppy' from *The Sunnyside* by A.A. Milne

Curtis Brown Ltd, New York and Atheneum Publishers for 'A Monstrous Mouse' from *One Winter Night in August and Other Nonsense Jingles* by X. J. Kennedy (a Margaret K. McElderry Book, copyright © 1975 by X. J. Kennedy); Curtis Brown Ltd, New York and Little Brown and Company, Boston for 'Bananas and Cream' and 'Jug and Mug' from *Every Time I Climb a Tree* by David McCord (copyright © 1961, 1962, 1967 by David McCord)

Andre Deutsch Limited for 'Horrible Things' from *Seen Grandpa Lately* (1972) by Roy Fuller; 'It was Spring in the Fields and Woods', 'I'm alone in the evening', 'Two Cats', 'Hog-pig waits on a mountain', 'Have you seen the Hidebehind?', 'It was a stormy night' and 'Down the Road' from *Mind Your Own Business* (1974) by Michael Rosen

Bananas and Cream

Bananas and Cream

Bananas and cream,
Bananas and cream:
All we could say was
Bananas and cream.

We couldn't say fruit,
We couldn't say cow,
We didn't say sugar –
We don't say it now.

Bananas and cream,
Bananas and cream,
All we could shout was
Bananas and cream.

We didn't say why,
We didn't say how;
We forgot it was fruit,
We forgot the old cow;
We *never* said sugar,
We only said WOW!

Bananas and cream,
Bananas and cream;
All that we want is
Bananas and cream!

We didn't say dish,
We didn't say spoon;
We said not tomorrow,
But NOW and HOW SOON

Bananas and cream,
Bananas and cream?
We yelled for bananas,
Bananas and scream!

David McCord

The Kettle

There's a little metal kettle
That is sitting near the settle.
You will hear the tittle-tattle
Of the lid begin to rattle
When the kettle starts to boil.
What a pretty prittle-prattle
Of the kettle near the settle,
Such a merry tittle-tattle
When the lid begins to rattle
And the kettle starts to boil.

Gwynneth Thurburn

Cow

'Cow' sounds heavy.
Cow
Standing in the meadow
Chewing.
A big fur box on legs
Mooing.

Karla Kuskin

Six Times One

Is six times one a lot of fun?
Or eight times two?
Perhaps for you.
But five times three
Unhinges me,
While six and seven and eight times eight
Put me in an awful state
And four and six and nine times nine
Make me want to cry and whine
So when I get to twelve times ten
I begin to wonder when
I can take a vacation from multiplication
And go out
And start playing again.

Karla Kuskin

Robert Rowley

Robert Rowley rolled a round roll round,
A round roll Robert Rowley rolled round.
Where rolled the round roll Robert Rowley rolled round?

Anon.

What is This Here?

With my hands on my head, what is this here?
This is my THINKER, right over here.
That's what I learned in school.

With my hands on my head, what is this here?
This is my I-SEE-YOU, right over here.
Thinker, I-see-you, hinky dinky do.
That's what I learned in school.

With my hands on my head, what is this here?
This is my SNEEZE-MAKER, right over here.
Thinker, I-see-you, sneeze-maker, hinky dinky do.
That's what I learned in school.

With my hands on my head, what is this here?
This is my SOUP STRAINER, right over here.
Thinker, I-see-you, sneeze-maker, soup strainer,
    hinky dinky do.
That's what I learned in school.

With my hands on my neck, what is this here?
This is my COLLAR HOLDER, right over here.
Thinker, I-see-you, sneeze-maker, soup strainer,
    collar holder, hinky dinky do.
That's what I learned in school.

With my hands on my body, what is this here?
This is my BREAD BASKET, right over here.
Thinker, I-see-you, sneeze-maker, soup strainer,
  collar holder, bread basket, hinky dinky do.
That's what I learned in school.

With my hands on my body, what is this here?
This is my BELT HOLDER, right over here.
Thinker, I-see-you, sneeze-maker, soup strainer,
  collar holder, bread basket, belt holder,
  hinky dinky do.
That's what I learned in school.

With my hands on my legs, what is this here?
This is my KNEE CAPPER, right over here.
Thinker, I-see-you, sneeze-maker, soup strainer,
  collar holder, bread basket, belt holder, knee
  capper, hinky dinky do.
That's what I learned in school.

With my hands on my feet, what is this here?
This is my SHOE HOLDER, right over here.
Thinker, I-see-you, sneeze-maker, soup strainer,
  collar holder, bread basket, belt holder, knee
  capper, shoe holder, hinky dinky do.
That's what I learned in school.

Anon.

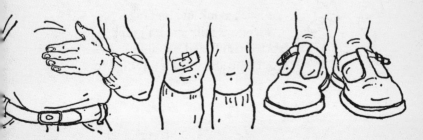

Jug and Mug

'Jug, aren't you fond of Mug?'
'Him I could hug,' said Jug.
'Mug, aren't you fond of Jug?'
'Him I could almost slug!'
'Humph,' said Jug with a shrug.
'When he pours, he goes *Glug*!' said Mug.
'Well, *I* don't spill on the rug,' said Jug.
'Smug old Jug,' said Mug.
'I'll fill you, Mug,' said Jug.
'*Will*, will you, Jug!' said Mug.
'Don't be ugly,' said Jug juggly.
'Big lug,' said Mug.
Glug.

David McCord

Who Am I ?

As black as ink and isn't ink,
As white as milk and isn't milk,
As soft as silk and isn't silk,
And hops about like a filly-foal.

Anon.

(A magpie)

Hello's a handy word

Hello's a handy word to say
At least a hundred times a day.
Without Hello what would I do
Whenever I bumped into you?
Without Hello where would you be
Whenever you bumped into me?
Hello's a handy word to know.
Hello Hello Hello Hello.

Mary Ann Hoberman

Good morning when it's morning

Good morning when it's morning
Good night when it is night
Good evening when it's dark out
Good day when it is light
Good morning to the sunshine
Good evening to the sky
And when it's time to go away
Good-bye
Good-bye
Good-bye.

Mary Ann Hoberman

What is Red?

Red is a sunset
Blazing and bright.
Red is feeling brave
With all your might.
Red is a sunburn
Spot on your nose.
Sometimes red
Is a red, red rose.
Red squiggles out
When you cut your hand.
Red is a brick and
The sound of a band.
Red is a hotness
You get inside
When you're embarrassed
And want to hide.
Firecracker, fire-engine
Fire-flicker red –
And when you're angry
Red runs through your head.
Red is an Indian,
A valentine heart,
The trimming on
A circus cart.

Red is a lipstick,
Red is a shout,
Red is a signal
That says: 'Watch out!'
Red is a great big
Rubber ball.
Red is the giant-est
Colour of all.
Red is a show-off
No doubt about it –
But can you imagine
Living without it?

Mary O'Neil

19

My Dame hath a Lame Tame Crane

My Dame hath a lame tame crane
My Dame hath a crane that is lame
Pray gentle Jane,
Let my Dame's lame tame crane
Feed and come home again.

Anon.

Ten hens

Ten hens
Nine lines
Eight plates
Seven elevens
Six picks
Five hives
Four doors
Three trees
Two shoes
AND ONE GREAT BIG BUN

Barbara Ireson

20

A Nonsense Alphabet

A   was an ape,
Who stole some white tape
And tied up his toes
In four beautiful bows.
                    a!
            Funny old Ape!

B   was a bat,
Who slept all the day
And fluttered about
When the sun went away.
                    b!
            Brown little Bat!

C   was a camel,
You rode on his hump
And if you fell off,
You came down such a bump!
                    c!
            What a high Camel!

D   was a dove
Who lived in a wood
With such pretty soft wings,
And so gentle and good.
                    d!
            Dear little Dove!

E was an eagle
Who sat on the rocks
And looked down on the fields
And the far away flocks.
e!
Beautiful Eagle!

F was a fan
Made of beautiful stuff
And when it was used
It went – Puffy-puff-puff!
f!
Nice little Fan!

G was a gooseberry
Perfectly red;
To be made into jam
And eaten with bread.
g!
Gooseberry red!

H was a heron
Who stood in a stream
The length of his neck
And his legs, was extreme.
h!
Long-legged Heron!

I was an inkstand
Which stood on a table
With a nice pen to write with,
When we were able!
i!
Neat little Inkstand!

J was a jug,
So pretty and white
With fresh water in it
At morning and night.
j!
Nice little Jug!

K was a kingfisher,
Quickly he flew
So bright and so pretty,
Green, purple and blue.
k!
Kingfisher, blue!

L was a lily
So white and so sweet
To see it and smell it
Was quite a nice treat!
l!
Beautiful Lily!

M was a man,
Who walked round and round,
And he wore a long coat
That came down to the ground.
m!
Funny old Man!

N was a nut
So smooth and so brown,
And when it was ripe
It fell tumble-dum-down.
n!
Nice little Nut!

O　was an oyster
Who lived in his shell,
If you left him alone
He felt perfectly well.
　　　o!
　　Open-mouthed Oyster!

P　was a polly
All red, blue and green
The most beautiful polly
That ever was seen.
　　　p!
　　Poor little Polly!

Q　was a quill
Made into a pen,
But I do not know where
And I cannot say when.
　　　q!
　　Nice little Quill!

R　was a rattlesnake
Rolled up so tight,
Those who saw him ran quickly
For fear he should bite.
　　　r!
　　Rattlesnake bite!

S　was a screw
To screw down a box
And then it was fastened
Without any locks.
　　　s!
　　Valuable Screw!

T   was a thimble
Of silver so bright
When placed on the finger
It fitted so tight!
t!
Nice little Thimble!

U   was an upper-coat
Woolly and warm
To wear over all
In the snow or the storm.
u!
What a nice Upper-coat!

V   was a veil
With a border upon it
And a riband to tie it
All round a pink bonnet.
v!
Pretty green Veil!

W   was a watch
Where in letters of gold
The hour of the day
You might always behold.
w!
Beautiful Watch!

X   was King Xerxes
Who wore on his head
A mighty large turban,
Green, yellow and red.
x!
Look at King Xerxes!

Y   was a yak
From the land of Thibet
Except his white tail
He was all black as jet.
y!
Look at the Yak!

Z   was a zebra,
All striped white and black,
And if he were tame
You might ride on his back.
z!
Pretty striped Zebra!

Edward Lear

What's in There?

What's in there?
  Gold and money.
Where's my share of it?
  The mouse ran away with it.
Where's the mouse?
  In her house.

Where's the house?
  In the wood.
Where's the wood?
  The fire burnt it.
Where's the fire?
  The water quenched it.

Where's the water?
  The brown bull drank it.
Where's the brown bull?
  At the back of Birnie's Hill.
Where's Birnie's Hill?
  All clad with snow.
Where's the snow?
  The sun melted it.
Where's the sun?
  High, high up in the air.

Anon.

There's a Hole in the Middle of the Sea

There's a hole, there's a hole, there's a hole in the middle of the sea.

There's a log in the hole in the middle of the sea.

There's a hole, there's a hole, there's a hole in the middle of the sea.

There's a bump on the log in the hole in the middle of the sea.

There's a hole, there's a hole, there's a hole in the middle of the sea.

There's a frog on the bump on the log in the hole in the middle of the sea.

There's a hole, there's a hole, there's a hole in the middle of the sea.

There's a fly on the frog on the bump on the log in the hole in the middle of the sea.

There's a hole, there's a hole, there's a hole in the middle of the sea.

There's a wing on the fly on the frog on the bump on the log in the hole in the middle of the sea.

There's a hole, there's a hole, there's a hole in the middle of the sea.

There's a flea on the wing on the fly on the frog on the bump on the log in the hole in the middle of the sea.

There's a hole, there's a hole, there's a hole in the middle of the sea.

Anon.

On the Ning Nang Nong

On the Ning Nang Nong
Where the Cows go Bong!
And the Monkeys all say Boo!
There's a Nong Nang Ning
Where the trees go Ping!
And the tea pots Jibber Jabber Joo.
On the Nong Ning Nang
All the mice go Clang!
And you just can't catch 'em when they do!
So it's Ning Nang Nong!
Cows go Bong!
Nong Nang Ning!
Trees go Ping!
Nong Ning Nang!
The mice go Clang!
What a noisy place to belong,
Is the Ning Nang Ning Nang Nong!!

Spike Milligan

The Mouse and the Fire Engines

Here is a house, a neat little place
With antimacassars and curtains of lace,
That stood in a street in Stirling.

Here is a mouse
That appeared in the house,
A neat little place
With curtains of lace
That stood in a street in Stirling.

Here is Miss Simpson who uttered a yell
As out of the house she rushed pell-mell
At the sight of the mouse
That appeared in her house,
A neat little place
With curtains of lace
That stood in a street in Stirling.

Here is a boy who sings in the choir
Running and waving and shouting 'Fire!'
When little Miss Simpson uttered a yell
As out of the house she rushed pell-mell
At the sight of the mouse
That appeared in her house,
A neat little place
With curtains of lace
That stood in a street in Stirling.

Here is a policeman on his beat,
Marching with dignity down the street,
Who met the boy who sings in the choir,
Running and waving and shouting 'Fire!'
When little Miss Simpson uttered a yell
As out of the house she rushed pell-mell
At the sight of the mouse
That appeared in her house,
A neat little place
With curtains of lace
That stood in a street in Stirling.

Here is the operator clearing the line
For somebody dialling 999;
For the dignified policeman went from his beat
To the telephone box at the end of the street
When he met the boy who sings in the choir,
Running and waving and shouting 'Fire!'
When little Miss Simpson uttered a yell
As out of the house she rushed pell-mell
At the sight of the mouse
That appeared in her house,
A neat little place
With curtains of lace
That stood in a street in Stirling.

Here are the fire engines, three or four,
Their bells are ringing, their engines roar;

For the telephone girl has cleared the line
For somebody dialling 999;
For the dignified policeman went from his beat
To the telephone box at the end of the street
When he met the boy who sings in the choir,
Running and waving and shouting 'Fire!'
When little Miss Simpson uttered a yell
As out of the house she rushed pell-mell
At the sight of the mouse
That appeared in her house,
A neat little place
With curtains of lace
That stood in a street in Stirling.

Here is Miss Simpson who, much upset,
Has a narrow escape from getting wet;
For the firemen propose
To turn on the hose,
Without pause to inquire
Whereabouts is the fire,
But Miss Simpson calls out at the very last minute
That this is *her* house and there's not a fire in it.
It's a neat little place
With curtains of lace
That stood in a street in Stirling.

Here are the firemen coiling their hose.
They jump on the engines and everyone goes,
Bicycles, cars and folk on their feet,
Even the policeman returns to his beat.
Then the boy and Miss Simpson search for the mouse,
From attic to cellar they ransack the house,
A neat little place
With curtains of lace
That stood in a street in Stirling.

Here is the magistrate frowning next day
And stating severely that someone must pay
For fire engines' petrol and firemen's wages,
And ferreting out by steps and stages
What is the name
Of the person to blame,
Wishful to find and to punish the same.
The policeman declared that he couldn't decline
To dial the number 999.
The choirboy explained how he made the mistake,
And little Miss Simpson, all of a quake,
Told of the mouse
That appeared in her house,
A neat little place
With curtains of lace
That stood in a street in Stirling.

At length the magistrate cleared his throat,
And first he said and then he wrote:
'The fire engines it seems were summoned in error,
Due to Miss Simpson's screams of terror;
So the mouse that caused them must bear the blame.
But, since no one can find and punish the same,
Stirling town council must pay the cost
And, doubtless, recover the money so lost
By raising the rates on each neat little place,
With antimacassars and curtains of lace,
That stands in the streets of Stirling.'

Wilma Horsbrugh

Weather Report

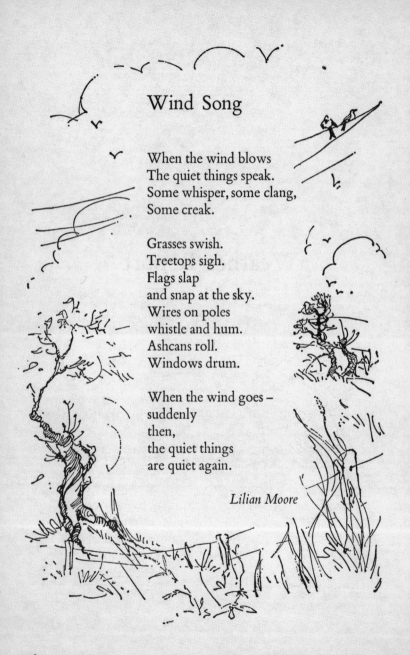

Wind Song

When the wind blows
The quiet things speak.
Some whisper, some clang,
Some creak.

Grasses swish.
Treetops sigh.
Flags slap
and snap at the sky.
Wires on poles
whistle and hum.
Ashcans roll.
Windows drum.

When the wind goes –
suddenly
then,
the quiet things
are quiet again.

Lilian Moore

It is grey out

It is grey out.
It is grey in.
In me
It is as grey as the day is grey.
The trees look sad
And I,
Not knowing why I do,
Cry.

Karla Kuskin

Dragon Smoke

Breathe and blow
white clouds
   with every puff.
It's cold today,
   cold enough
to see your breath.
Huff!
   Breathe dragon smoke
   today!

Lilian Moore

Down the Road

Down the road
we see behind wet windows
eyes up
trying to pull the clouds apart.
Before they come out again
they want to see dry islands on the paving-stones
and the drips from the bricks go warm.

We're listening to Niagara in the drains
and camping in Cape Horn under the butcher's awning.
We change guard at the tobacconist
watch petrol rainbows in the gutter.
A dog droops there
wishing he had a sou'wester on;
and like our ball hitting the chicken-wire
as he shudders his body
he makes a show of his own rain too.

Michael Rosen

The Wind

The wind stood up, and gave a shout;
He whistled on his fingers, and

Kicked the withered leaves about,
And thumped the branches with his hand,

And said he'll kill, and kill, and kill;
And so he will! And so he will!

James Stephens

Windy Nights

Rumbling in the chimneys,
   Rattling at the doors,
Round the roofs and round the roads
   The rude wind roars;
Raging through the darkness,
   Raving through the trees,
Racing off again across
   The great grey seas.

Rodney Bennett

Rain Sizes

Rain comes in various sizes.
Some rain is as small as a mist.
It tickles your face with surprises,
And tingles as if you'd been kissed.

Some rain is the size of a sprinkle
And doesn't put out all the sun.
You can see the drops sparkle and twinkle,
And a rainbow comes out when it's done.

Some rain is as big as a nickel
And comes with a crash and a hiss.
It comes down too heavy to tickle.
It's more like a splash than a kiss.

When it rains the right size and you're wrapped in
Your rainclothes, it's fun out of doors.
But run home before you get trapped in
The big rain that rattles and roars.

John Ciardi

Rain

I opened my eyes
And looked up at the rain
And it dripped in my head
And flowed into my brain
So pardon this wild crazy thing I just said
I'm just not the same since there's rain in my head.
I step very softly
I walk very slow
I can't do a hand-stand
Or I might overflow.
And all I can hear as I lie in my bed
Is the slishity-slosh of the rain in my head.

Shel Silverstein

The Rain

The rain is raining all around,
It falls on field and tree;
It rains on the umbrellas here
And on the ships at sea.

Robert Louis Stevenson

Days that the wind takes over

Days that the wind takes over
Blowing through the gardens
Blowing birds out of the street trees
Blowing cats around corners
Blowing my hair out
Blowing my heart apart
Blowing high in my head
Like the sea sound caught in a shell.
One child put her thin arms around the wind
And they went off together.
Later the wind came back
Alone.

Karla Kuskin

Thunder

I hear thunder.
I hear thunder.
Hark ! Don't you?
Hark ! Don't you?
Pitter-patter, raindrops,
Pitter-patter, raindrops,
I'm wet through,
So are you.

Anon.

Week of Winter Weather

On Monday icy rain poured down
and flooded drains all over town.

Tuesday's gales rent elm and ash;
dead branches came down with a crash.

On Wednesday bursts of hail and sleet:
no-one walked along our street.

Thursday stood out clear and calm
but the sun was paler than my arm.

Friday's frost that bit your ears
was cold enough to freeze your tears.

Saturday's sky was ghostly grey;
we smashed ice on the lake today.

Christmas Eve was Sunday and
snow fell like foam across the land.

Wes Magee

Who?

Who's been
criss-
crossing
this
fresh snow?

Well, Rabbit was here.
How did he go?
Hop-hopping.
Stopping.
Hopping away.

A deer
stood near
this tall young tree.
Took three steps.
(What did she see?)
Didn't stay.
(What did she hear?)

Fox brushed snow dust
from a bush.
Squirrel, too.
But who –
WHO
walked on TWO legs
here
today?

Lilian Moore

Go Wind

Go wind, blow
Push wind, swoosh.
  Shake things
  take things
  make things
    fly.

  Rings things
  swing things
  fling things
    high.

Go wind, blow
Push things . . . wheee.
  No, wind, no.
  Not me –
  not *me*.

        Lilian Moore

Little Wind

Little wind, blow on the hill-top,
  Little wind, blow down the plain;
Little wind, blow up the sunshine,
  Little wind, blow off the rain.

        Kate Greenaway

Rain

Rain on the green grass,
And rain on the tree,
And rain on the house-top,
But not upon me!

Anon.

Wet

Wet wet wet
the world of melting winter,
icicles weeping themselves away
on the eaves
little brown rivers streaming
down the road
nibbling
at the edges of the tired snow,
   all puddled mud
   not a dry place to put
   a booted foot,
everything
   dripping
   slipping
   gushing
   slushing
and listen to that brook,
rushing
like a puppy loosed from its leash.

Lilian Moore

White Fields

In the winter time we go
Walking in the fields of snow;

Where there is no grass at all;
Where the top of every wall,

Every fence, and every tree
Is as white as white can be.

Pointing out the way we came –
Every one of them the same –

All across the fields there be
Prints in silver filligree;

And our mothers always know,
By the footprints in the snow,

Where it is the children go.

James Stephens

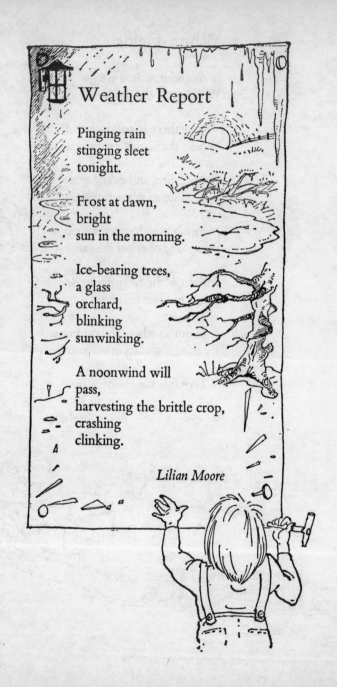

Weather Report

Pinging rain
stinging sleet
tonight.

Frost at dawn,
bright
sun in the morning.

Ice-bearing trees,
a glass
orchard,
blinking
sunwinking.

A noonwind will
pass,
harvesting the brittle crop,
crashing
clinking.

Lilian Moore

Time to Get Up

Waking

My secret way of waking
is like a place
to hide.
I'm very still,
my eyes are shut.
They all think I am sleeping
but
I'm wide awake inside.

They all think I am sleeping
but
I'm wiggling my toes.
I feel sun-fingers
on my cheek.
I hear voices whisper-speak.
I squeeze my eyes
to keep them shut
so they will think I'm sleeping
BUT
I'm really wide awake inside
– and no one knows!

Lilian Moore

Time to Get Up

A bird who had a yellow bill
Landed on my window sill,
Winked his shining eye and said,
'Time to get up, Sleepy Head!'

Robert Louis Stevenson

Porridge is bubbling

Porridge is bubbling,
Bubbling hot,
Stir it round
And round in the pot.
The bubbles plip!
The bubbles plop!
It's ready to eat
All bubbling hot.

Anon.

The Dustbin Men

The older ones have gone to school,
My breakfast's on the plate,
But I can't leave the window-pane,
I might be just too late.

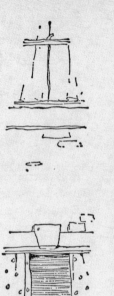

I've heard the clatter down the street,
I know they're creeping near,
The team of gruff-voiced, burly men
Who keep our dustbins clear.

And I must watch and see them clang
The dustbins on the road,
And stand in pairs to heave up high
The double-handled load.

Yes, there they come, the lorry growls
And grinds in bottom gear;
The dustman knees the garden gate
As, high up by his ear,
Firmly he balances the bin,
Head tilted to one side;
The great mouth of the rubbish cart
Is yawning very wide;
To me the mouth looks like a beast's
A dragon's hungry jaws
That snap the refuse out of sight
Behind those sliding doors.

The lorry-dragon every day
Is in a ravenous mood,
And cardboard boxes, bottles, jars
Are all part of his food.

He gobbles up old magazines,
Saucepans and broken jugs
Pieces of red linoleum,
And dirty, tufted rugs.

He crunches shattered pictures,
Old bicycles and tyres,
A bird-cage with its seed-tray,
Its bell and rusty wires;

And fractured clocks and mirrors,
A rocking-chair and broom,
A mattress and an iron bed;
Where does he find the room?

And like a dragon sated,
His great maw crammed quite tight,
He lifts his head and swallows
His breakfast out of sight.

What would the careless people
Who clutter up the street
Do without hungry dragons
To keep our houses neat?

Gregory Harrison

Summer Goes

Summer goes, summer goes
Like the sand between my toes
When the waves go out.
That's how summer pulls away,
Leaves me standing here today,
Waiting for the school bus.

Summer brought, summer brought
All the frogs that I have caught,
Frogging at the pond,
Hot dogs, flowers, shells and rocks,
Postcards in my postcard box –
Places far away.

Summer took, summer took
All the lessons in my book,
Blew them far away.
I forgot the things I knew –
Arithmetic and spelling too,
Never thought about them.

Summer's gone, summer's gone –
Fall and winter coming on,
Frosty in the morning.
Here's the school bus right on time.
I'm not really sad that I'm
Going back to school.

Russell Hoban

Betty and I

Betty my sister and I fell out,
And what do you think it was all about?
She loved coffee and I loved tea,
And that was the reason we could not agree.

Anon.

As I was going along

As I was going along, long, long,
A-singing a comical song, song, song,
The lane that I went was so long, long, long,
And the song that I sang was so long, long, long,
That the words and the music went wrong, wrong, wrong,
As I went singing along!

Anon.

At the Seaside

When I was down beside the sea
A wooden spade they gave to me
    To dig the sandy shore.

My holes were empty like a cup.
In every hole the sea came up
    Till it could come no more.

Robert Louis Stevenson

Skipping Song

When bread-and-cheese
   on hawthorn trees
makes buds of tiny green;
When big dogs chase
   around, and little
dogs run in between;
When shouts and songs
   and arguments
are heard on every lip;
Then is the time
   when all true-minded
children want to skip.
To-skip-skip-skip-skip-skip-skip-skip.
The-time-when-all-the-children-want-to-skip.

When days grow long,
   and sister Jean
with Bobby Bates goes walking;
   When steps are warm
   for sitting on,
and pavements dry for chalking;
When last year's summer
   frocks come out,
and thrill with summer hope;
Then is the time
   to search the house
and find a piece of rope.
It's-the-time-time-time-time-time-time-time-
to-search-the-house-and-find-a-piece-of-rope.

There's skipping ropes
   so thin and light
it's hard to twirl them round;
There's hairy ropes with
   knots, and heavy
ropes that slap the ground;
And bits of plastic
   washing line
are there among the rest;
But of all the ropes
   the rope with painted
handles is the best.
It's-the-best-best-best-best-best-best-best.
The rope with painted handles is the best –
THAT'S MINE.

John Walsh

Whip Top

Whip top! Whip top!
Turn about and never stop!
Monday's top will spin away,
Tuesday's top will sing all day,
Wednesday's top is never slow,
Thursday's top to sleep will go,
Friday's top will dance about,
Saturday's top will tire you out!
Whip top! Whip top!
Spin around and never stop!

Anon.

Me, myself, and I

Me, myself, and I –
We went to the kitchen and ate a pie.
Then my mother she came in
And chased us out with a rolling pin.

Anon.

The Tidy Child

My little broom is made of twigs
Tied round and round with bright green string,
With it, on windy autumn days
   I do my tidying.

I sweep and sweep the yellow leaves
That tumble from our great oak tree,
And when I sit down for a rest
   They tumble on to me.

Barbara Baker

Pancake Day

Mummy made pancakes on Tuesday,
She tossed them in the air,
One fell on the table,
Two fell on the chair,
One fell on the cooker
And one fell in the grate,
But, lucky for me,
I had three
Because they fell on my plate.

Shaun Fountain

Drinking Fountain

When I climb up
  To get a drink,
It doesn't work
  The way you'd think.

I turn it up.
  The water goes
And hits me right
  Upon the nose.

I turn it down
  To make it small
And don't get any
  Drink at all.

Marchette Chute

The Old Field

The old field is sad
Now the children have gone home.
They have played with him all afternoon,
Kicking the ball to him, and him
Kicking it back.

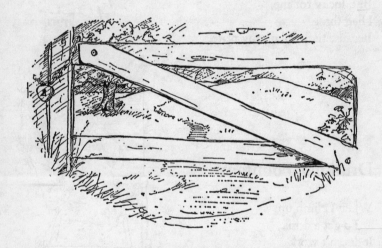

But now it is growing cold and dark.
He thinks of their warm breath, and their
Feet like little hot-water bottles.
A bit rough, some of them, but still . . .

And now, he thinks, there's not even a dog
To tickle me.
The gates are locked.
The birds don't like this nasty sneaking wind,
And nor does he.

D. J. Enright

I'm alone in the evening

I'm alone in the evening
when the family sits
reading and sleeping,
and I watch the fire in close
to see flame goblins
wriggling out of their caves
for the evening

Later I'm alone
when the bath has gone cold around me
and I have put my foot
beneath the cold tap
where it can dribble
through valleys between my toes
out across the white plain of my foot
and bibble bibble into the sea

I'm alone
when mum's switched out the light
my head against the pillow
listening to ca thump ca thump
in the middle of my ears.
It's my heart.

Michael Rosen

After a Bath

After my bath
I try, try, try
to wipe myself
till I'm dry, dry, dry.

Hands to wipe
and fingers and toes
and two wet legs
and a shiny nose.

Just think how much
less time I'd take
if I were a dog
and could shake, shake, shake.

Aileen Fisher

The Falling Star

I saw a star slide down the sky,
Blinding the north as it went by,
Too lovely to be bought or sold,
Too burning and too quick to hold,
Good only to make wishes on
And then forever to be gone.

Sara Teasdale

February Twilight

I stood beside a hill
   Smooth with new-laid snow,
A single star looked out
   From the cold evening glow.

There was no other creature
   That saw what I could see –
I stood and watched the evening star
   As long as it watched me.

                Sara Teasdale

Last Song

To the Sun
Who has shone
   All day,
To the Moon
Who has gone
   Away,
To the milk-white
Silk-white,
Lily-white Star,
A fond good-night
Wherever you are.

    James Guthrie

Roll Over

There were ten in the bed
And the little one said:
  'Roll over! Roll over!'
So they all rolled over,
And one fell out.

There were nine in the bed
And the little one said:
  'Roll over! Roll over!'
So they all rolled over,
And one fell out.

There were eight in the bed
And the little one said:
  'Roll over! Roll over!'
So they all rolled over
And one fell out.

There were seven in the bed
And the little one said:
  'Roll over! Roll over!'
So they all rolled over,
And one fell out.

There were six in the bed
And the little one said:
  'Roll over! Roll over!'
So they all rolled over,
And one fell out.

There were five in the bed
And the little one said:
  'Roll over! Roll over!'
So they all rolled over,
And one fell out.

There were four in the bed
And the little one said:
  'Roll over! Roll over!'
So they all rolled over,
And one fell out.

There were three in the bed
And the little one said:
  'Roll over! Roll over!'
So they all rolled over,
And one fell out.

There were two in the bed
And the little one said:
  'Roll over! Roll over!'
So they all rolled over,
And one fell out.

There was one in the bed
And the little one said:
  'Roll over! Roll over!'
So HE rolled over,
And HE fell out.

So there was the bed –
And no one said:
  'Roll over! Roll over!'

Anon.

Night-lights

There is no need to light a night-light
On a light night like tonight;
For a night-light's light's a slight light
When the moonlight's white and bright.

Anon.

Moon – Come – Out

Moon – Come – Out
And Sun – Go – In,
Here's a soft blanket
To cuddle your chin.

Moon – Go – In
And Sun – Come – Out,
Throw off the blanket
And bustle about.

Eleanor Farjeon

What the Leaves Said

The Leaves are Green

The leaves are green
The nuts are brown,
They hang so high
They will not come down.

Leave them alone
Till frosty weather,
Then they will all
Come down together.

Anon.

Autumn

Yellow the bracken,
Golden the sheaves,
Rosy the apples,
Crimson the leaves;
Mist on the hillside,
Clouds grey and white.
Autumn, good morning!
Summer, good night.

Florence Hoatson

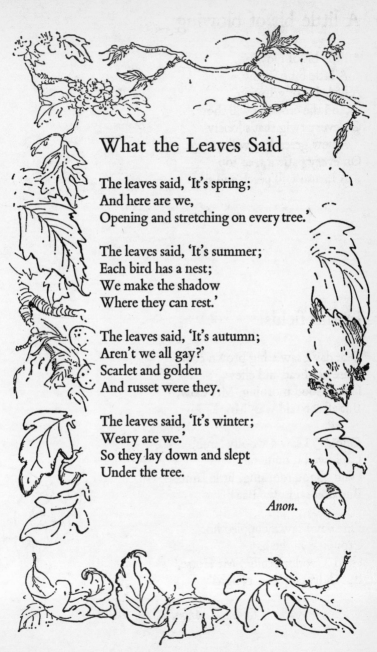

What the Leaves Said

The leaves said, 'It's spring;
And here are we,
Opening and stretching on every tree.'

The leaves said, 'It's summer;
Each bird has a nest;
We make the shadow
Where they can rest.'

The leaves said, 'It's autumn;
Aren't we all gay?'
Scarlet and golden
And russet were they.

The leaves said, 'It's winter;
Weary are we.'
So they lay down and slept
Under the tree.

Anon.

A little bit of blowing

A little bit of blowing,
  A little bit of snow,
A little bit of growing,
  And the crocuses will show;
On every twig that's lonely
  A new green leaf will spring;
On every patient tree-top
  A thrush will perch and sing.

Anon.

In the fields

One day I saw a big brown cow
Raise her head and chew,
I said 'Good morning, Mrs Cow,'
But all she said was 'Moo!'

One day I saw a woolly lamb,
I followed it quite far,
I said 'Good morning, little lamb,'
But all it said was 'Baa!'

One day I saw a dappled horse
Cropping in the hay,
I said 'Good morning, Mr Horse,'
But all he said was 'Neigh!'

Anon.

On the Farm

I went to visit a farm one day
And saw a pig across the way.
Now what do you think I heard it say?

OINK, OINK, OINK.

I went to visit a farm one day
And saw a sheep across the way.
Now what do you think I heard it say?

BAA, BAA, BAA.

I went to visit a farm one day
And saw a cow across the way.
Now what do you think I heard it say?

MOO, MOO, MOO.

Anon.

Earth-worm

Do
you
squirm
when
you
see
an earth-worm?
I never
do squirm
because I think
a big fat worm
is really rather clever
the way it can shrink
and go
so small
without
a sound
into the ground.
And then
what about
all
that
work it does
and no oxygen
or miner's hat?
Marvellous
you have to admit,
even if you don't like fat

pink worms a bit,
how with that
thin
slippery skin
it makes its way
day after day
through the soil,
such honest toil.
And don't forget
the dirt
it eats, I bet
you wouldn't like to come out
at night to squirt
it all over the place
with no eyes in your face:
I doubt
too if you know
an earth-worm is deaf, but
it can hear YOU go
to and fro
even if you cut
it in half,
do not laugh
or squirm
again
when
you
suddenly
see
a worm.

Leonard Clark

Yellow Weed

How did you get here,
weed?
Who brought your seed?

Did it lift
on the wind and
sail
and drift
from a far and yellow
field?

Was your seed a
burr,
a sticky burr that
clung to a
fox's
furry tail?

Did it fly with a
bird
who liked to feed
on the tasty
seed
of the yellow
weed?
How did you come?

Lilian Moore

74

Seed Song

This is a story about a seed
Lying in the ground
Which slept right through the wintertime
Till Springtime came around.

When all at once the sunshine came
And drops of gentle rain,
The ground became much warmer
And the seed woke up again.

Then from the seed there grew a root
Which wriggled in the ground;
Root from the seed,
That wonderful seed
Way down in the ground.

Then from the root there came a shoot
Which came up for some air;
Shoot from the root,
Root from the seed
That wonderful seed
Way down in the ground.

Then from the shoot there came a leaf
When the sun began to shine;
Leaf from the shoot,
Shoot from the root,
Root from the seed,
That wonderful seed
Way down in the ground.

Then from the leaf there came a plant
Watered by the roots;
Plant from the leaf,
Leaf from the shoot,
Shoot from the root,
Root from the seed,
That wonderful seed
Way down in the ground.

Then from the plant there came a bud
As summer came around;
Bud from the plant,
Plant from the leaf,
Leaf from the shoot,
Shoot from the root,

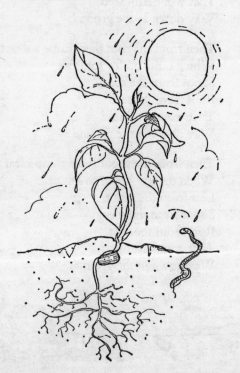

Root from the seed,
That wonderful seed
Way down in the ground.

Then from the bud there grew a flower
To greet the summer sun;
Flower from the bud,
Bud from the plant,
Plant from the leaf,
Leaf from the shoot,
Shoot from the root,
Root from the seed,
That wonderful seed
Way down in the ground.

But when at last the Autumn came
And leaves fell all around,
A new seed ripened in the flower
And then dropped to the ground.
The seed slipped back into the earth
Washed by the gentle rain
And slept right through the wintertime
Till Spring came around again.

Christopher Rowe

The Hills

Sometimes I think the hills
That loom across the harbour
Lie there like sleeping dragons,
Crouched one above another,
With trees for tufts of fur
Growing all up and down
The ridges and humps of their backs,
And orange cliffs for claws
Dipped in the sea below.
Sometimes a wisp of smoke
Rises out of the hollows,
As if in their dragon sleep
They dreamed of strange old battles.

What if the hills should stir
Some day and stretch themselves,
Shake off the clinging trees
And all the clustered houses?

Rachel Field

It was Spring in the Fields

It was spring in the fields and woods
the leaves in the hedges shook in the wind
as a crow stood quite still on a white horse's back.
He was looking at the grass about him
and the trees at the edge of the paddock
when all of a sudden he said to the horse beneath his feet:
Do you see how green everything is today?
and the horse said:
well to tell you the truth – no, I don't.
everything looks pink to me
you see my eyes are pink . . . he stopped.
the crow spoke again:
Oh. I'm sorry.
But how do you know that everything you see is pink
when it's the only colour you've ever seen?
The horse sat thinking about that for a while
and then said:
well of course it's quite true what you say.
In fact I was only guessing.
But you see – when I was born,
everybody pointed at me and said: look at him –
his eyes are pink. So I thought everything I saw
was pink. It seemed a sensible thing to do at the time
The crow shook his head slowly to and fro
breathed in deeply and sympathetically
and flew off to make his nest in the clear green sky.

Michael Rosen

I know a little pussy

I know a little pussy,
Her coat is silver grey;
She lives down in the meadow,
Not very far away.
Although she is a pussy,
She'll never be a cat,
For she's a pussy willow –
Now what do you think of that?

Anon.

In the Wood

Cold winter's in the wood,
  I saw him pass
Crinkling up fallen leaves
  Along the grass.

Bleak winter's in the wood,
  The birds have flown
Leaving the naked trees
  Shivering alone.

King Winter's in the wood,
  I saw him go
Crowned with a coronet
  Of crystal snow.

Eileen Mathias

The Intruder

Two-boots in the forest walks,
Pushing through the bracken stalks.

Vanishing like a puff of smoke,
Nimbletail flies up the oak.

Longears helter-skelter shoots
Into his house among the roots.

At work upon the highest bark,
Tapperbill knocks off to hark.

Painted-wings through sun and shade
Flounces off along the glade.

Not a creature lingers by,
When clumping Two-boots comes to pry.

James Reeves

Three Little Girls

Three little girls were sitting on a rail,
    Sitting on a rail,
    Sitting on a rail;
Three little girls were sitting on a rail,
  On a fine hot day in September.

What did they talk about that fine day,
    That fine day,
    That fine day?
What did they talk about that fine day,
  That fine hot day in September?

The crows and the corn they talked about,
    Talked about,
    Talked about;
But nobody knows what was said by the crows,
  On that fine hot day in September.

Kate Greenaway

If I were an apple

If I were an apple
And grew upon a tree,
I think I'd fall down
On a good boy like me.
I wouldn't stay there
Giving nobody joy;
I'd fall down at once
And say, 'Eat me, my boy.'

Anon.

Time to go Home

Time to go home!
  Says the great steeple clock.
Time to go home!
  Says the gold weathercock.
Down sinks the sun
  In the valley to sleep;
Lost are the orchards
  In blue shadows deep.
Soft falls the dew
  On cornfield and grass;
Through the dark trees
  The evening airs pass:
Time to go home,
  They murmur and say;
Birds to their homes
  Have all flown away.
Nothing shines now
  But the gold weathercock.
Time to go home!
  Says the great steeple clock.

James Reeves

At Night

The grey owl hunts when the moon is bright,
He hunts and he hoots all through the night.
The black mole digs when the moon is strong,
He scrabbles with his sharp paws all night long.
And when the moon has gone and the sky is black,
Creeping through the woods comes old Poacher Jack.

Barbara Ireson

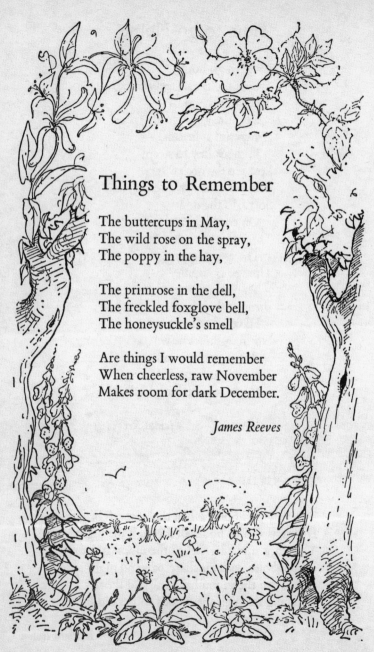

Things to Remember

The buttercups in May,
The wild rose on the spray,
The poppy in the hay,

The primrose in the dell,
The freckled foxglove bell,
The honeysuckle's smell

Are things I would remember
When cheerless, raw November
Makes room for dark December.

James Reeves

Bring on the Clowns

Please to Remember

Here am I,
A poor old Guy:
Legs in a bonfire,
Head in the sky;

Shoeless my toes,
Wild stars behind,
Smoke in my nose,
And my eye-peeps blind;

Old hat, old straw –
In this disgrace;
While the wildfire gleams
On a mask for face.

Ay, all I am made of
Only trash is;
And soon – soon,
Will be dust and ashes.

Walter de la Mare

The Foolish Man

I knew a man who always wore
A saucepan on his head.
I asked him what he did it for –
'I don't know why,' he said.
'It always makes my ears so sore;
I am a foolish man.
I should have left it off before
And worn a frying pan.'

Christopher Chamberlain

The Cobbler

Walking through the town one day,
I peeped in a window over the way;
And putting his needle through and through,
There sat the cobbler making a shoe.
For the world, he cares never the whisk of a broom,
All he wants is elbow room.
  Rap-a-tap-tap, tick-a-tack-too –
That is the way to make a shoe.

Anon.

Here Comes a Knight

Here comes a knight a-riding,
To the castle he has come;
The Lady Anne puts out her head;
My Lord is not at home.

There's no one but the children
And chickens in the pen;
The knight upon his charger
He says to Lady Anne:

And are the children naughty,
Or are the children good?
Oh very bad indeed, says she,
They won't do as they should.

Says he: then I'll not have them,
No use are they to me –
He turns him to the rightabout
And home again rides he.

Rose Fyleman

Peter, Peter, Pumpkin-Eater

Mrs Piper, tiny mite,
Had a giant's appetite;
She, as short as winter grass is,
Ate enough for twenty horses.
No, not even Humpty-Dumpty
Had so stretch-able a tumpty.
She ate so much when food was cheap
There wasn't any time to sleep;
When food was dear she slept all day
Or else, for lack, she pined away.
Peter, ere she'd vanished quite,
Found a pumpkin for his wife
Growing in a field alone.
He hollowed it into a home,
With door and window, leafy shutters,
Straw for pipes (in half for gutters).
Here they lived, whatever weather,
Long and happily together.
Fog or sunshine, storm or drizzle,
Peter sang while Mrs nibbled.
She never ate the pumpkin through –
The more she ate the more it grew.
Now, to end with, here's the song
That Peter sang – it isn't long:

Peter, Peter, Pumpkin-eater,
Had a wife and couldn't keep her.
He put her in a pumpkin shell
And there he kept her very well.

Ian Serraillier

Have you ever . . . ?

Have you ever heard
Of the wiggle-waggle waggon
With greedy Gregory sitting on the box?

Nobody can beat
What Gregory can eat.

A cow and a calf,
A horse and a half,
An ox and a steer,
Seven casks of beer,
Seventeen hares,
A shipload of pears,
A churchful of sheep . . .
And even then Gregory's so hungry he can't sleep!

Rose Fyleman

Two People

Two people live in Rosamund,
    And one is very nice;
The other is devoted
    To every kind of vice –

To walking where the puddles are,
    And eating far too quick,
And saying words she shouldn't know,
    And wanting spoons to lick.

Two people live in Rosamund,
    And one (I say it twice)
Is very nice *and* very good:
    The other's only nice.

E. V. Rieu

Jonathan

Jonathan Gee
Went out with his cow
He climbed up a tree
And sat on a bough.
He sat on a bough
And it broke in half,
And John's old cow
Did nothing but laugh.

Rose Fyleman

Alone in the Grange

Strange,
Strange,
Is the little old man
Who lives in the Grange.
Old,
Old;
And they say that he keeps
A box full of gold.
Bowed,
Bowed,
Is his thin little back
That once was so proud.
Soft,
Soft,
Are his steps as he climbs
The stairs to the loft.
Black,
Black,
Is the old shuttered house.
Does he sleep on a sack?

They say he does magic,
That he can cast spells,
That he prowls round the garden
Listening for bells;
That he watches for strangers,
Hates every soul,
And peers with his dark eye
Through the keyhole.

I wonder, I wonder,
As I lie in my bed,
Whether he sleeps with his hat on his head?
Is he really magician
With altar of stone
Or a lonely old gentleman
Left on his own?

Gregory Harrison

The Old Wives

Two old wives sat a-talking,
A-talking, a-talking, a-talking;
Two old wives sat a-talking
About the wind and weather –
Till their two old heads fell a-nodding,
A-nodding, a-nodding, a-nodding,
Till their two old heads fell a-nodding,
Their two old heads together.

Anon.

Proud Janey

Look at Janey coming down the street
THUMP! go the clogs upon her feet.
O, thumpety, thumpety, thump!

Look at the hat she wears on her head,
Better with a plant pot there instead.
O, thumpety, thumpety, thump!

Look at her shawl without a doubt,
It must be a dish cloth inside out.
O, thumpety, thumpety, thump!

Look at the way she walks along,
Just like a duck with its toes turned wrong.
O, thumpety, thumpety, THUMP!

Anon.

I had a little brother

I had a little brother
His name was Tiny Tim
I put him in the bathtub
To teach him how to swim
He drank up all the water
He ate up all the soap
He died last night
With a bubble in his throat
In came the doctor
In came the nurse
In came the lady
With the alligator purse
Out went the doctor
Out went the nurse
Out went the lady
With the alligator purse.

Anon.

My Sister Laura

My sister Laura's bigger than me
And lifts me up quite easily.
I can't lift her, I've tried and tried;
She must have something heavy inside.

Spike Milligan

Old John Muddlecombe

Old John Muddlecombe lost his cap,
He couldn't find it anywhere, the poor old chap.
He walked down the High Street, and everybody said,
'Silly John Muddlecombe, you've got it on your head!'

Anon.

Maggie

There was a small maiden named Maggie,
Whose dog was enormous and shaggy;
  The front end of him
  Looked vicious and grim –
But the tail end was friendly and waggy.

Anon.

There Was an Old Man of Toulon

There was an Old Man of Toulon
Who never had anything on.
  When they said: 'Wear some clothes!'
  He inquired: 'What are those?'
So they chased that man out of Toulon.

William Jay Smith

Horrible Things

'What's the horriblest thing you've seen?'
Said Nell to Jean.

'Some grey-coloured, trodden-on plasticine;
On a plate, a left-over cold baked bean;
A cloak-room ticket numbered thirteen;
A slice of meat without any lean;
The smile of a spiteful fairy-tale queen;
A thing in the sea like a brown submarine;
A cheese fur-coated in brilliant green;
A bluebottle perched on a piece of sardine.
What's the horriblest thing *you've* seen?'
Said Jean to Nell.

'Your face, as you tell
Of all the horriblest things you've seen.'

Roy Fuller

Walter Spaggot

Walter Spaggot, strange old man,
Does things wrong-ways-round,
Like back-to-front or in-side-out,
Or even up-side-down.

He puffs his pipe inside his ear,
Has glasses for his mouth,
And if he wants to travel North
Walks backwards to the South.

He comes from where he never is
And goes to where he's been,
He scrubs his shirt in the bath-tub
And baths in his washing-machine.

Walter Spaggot, strange old man,
Does things wrong-ways-round,
Like back-to-front or in-side-out,
Or even up-side-down.

(Funny old man.)

Peter Wesley-Smith

Skinny Winny

Skinny Winny,
Silly ninny,
Took a bath.

Pulled the plug.

Glug glug glug.

Question:
What do you think
happened to
Skinny Winny?

Peter Wesley-Smith

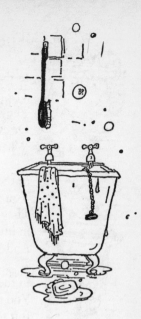

Too Polite

Broad met Stout
At the gate, and each
Was too polite to brush past.
'After you!' said Broad.
'After you!' said Stout.
They got in a dither
And went through together
And both
    stuck
      fast.

Ian Serraillier

The Land of the Bumbley Boo

In the Land of the Bumbley Boo
The people are red white and blue,
They never blow noses,
Or ever wear closes;
What a sensible thing to do!

In the Land of the Bumbley Boo
You can buy Lemon pie at the Zoo;
They give away Foxes
In little Pink Boxes
And Bottles of Dandelion Stew.

In the Land of the Bumbley Boo
You never see a Gnu,
But thousands of cats
Wearing trousers and hats
Made of Pumpkins and Pelican Glue!

Oh, the Bumbley Boo! the Bumbley Boo!
That's the place for me and you!
So hurry! Let's run!
The train leaves at one!
For the Land of the Bumbley Boo!
The wonderful Bumbley Boo-Boo-Boo!
The Wonderful Bumbley BOO!!!

Spike Milligan

The Plug-Hole Man

I know you're down there, Plug-hole Man,
  In the dark so utter,
For when I let the water out
  I hear you gasp and splutter.

And though I peer and peek and pry
  I've never seen you yet:
(I know you're down there, Plug-hole Man
  In your home so wet).

But you will not be there for long
  For I've a *plan*, you see;
I'm going to catch you, Plug-hole Man,
  And Christian's helping me.

We'll fill the bath with water hot,
  Then give the plug a heave,
And rush down to the outside drain –
  And *catch* you as you leave!

Carey Blyton

Night Starvation or The Biter Bit

At night, my Uncle Rufus
(Or so I've heard it said)
Would put his teeth into a glass
Of water by his bed.

At three o'clock one morning
He woke up with a cough,
And as he reached out for his teeth –
They bit his hand right off.

Carey Blyton

Witch, Witch

'Witch, witch, where do you fly?' . . .
'Under the clouds and over the sky.'

'Witch, witch, what do you eat?' . . .
'Little black apples from Hurricane Street.'

'Witch, witch, what do you drink?' . . .
'Vinegar, blacking and good red ink.'

'Witch, witch, where do you sleep?' . . .
'Up in the clouds where pillows are cheap.'

Rose Fyleman

Skilly Oogan

Skilly Oogan's no one you can see,
And no one else can be his friend but me,
Skilly lives where swallows live, away up high
Beneath the topmost eaves against the sky.
When all the world's asleep on moonlit nights
Up on our roof he flies his cobweb kites.
He has an acorn boat that, when it rains,
He sails in gutters, even down the drains.
Sometimes he hides in letters that I write –
Snug in the envelope and out of sight,
On six-cent stamps he travels in all weathers
And with the midnight owl returns on silent feathers.
In summer time he rides the dragonflies
Above the pond, and looks in bullfrogs' eyes
For his reflection when he combs his hair.
And sometimes when I want him he's not there;
But mostly Skilly Oogan's where I think he'll be,
And no one even knows his name but me.

Russell Hoban

Bring on the Clowns

Bring on the clowns!
Bring on the clowns!
Clowns wearing knickers
and clowns
wearing gowns.

Tall clowns and short clowns and skinny and fat,
a flat-footed clown with a jumping-jack hat.
A clown walking under a portable shower,
getting all wet just to water a flower.
A barefoot buffoon with balloons on his toes,
a clown with a polka-dot musical nose.
Clowns wearing teapots and clowns sporting plumes,
a clown with a tail made of brushes and brooms.

A balancing clown on a wobbly wheel,
seventeen clowns in an automobile.
Two jesters on pogo sticks dressed up in kilts,
pursuing a prankster escaping on stilts.
A sad-looking clown with a face like a tramp,
a clown with his stomach lit up like a lamp.
How quickly a clown can coax smiles out of frowns!
Make way for the merriment . . . bring on the clowns!

Jack Prelutsky

The famous Human Cannonball

The famous human cannonball
stands at the cannon's side.
He's very round and very small
and very dignified.

He bows to the east, he bows to the west,
he bows to the north and south,
then proudly puffing up his chest
he steps to the cannon's mouth.

The famous human cannonball
is ready to begin.
His helpers hoist him at his call
and gently stuff him in.
The air is filled with 'ahh's' and 'ohh's'
preparing for the thrill,
but when his helpers light the fuse
the audience is still.

Then in the hushed and darkened hall
the mighty cannon roars,
the famous human cannonball
shoots out and swiftly soars.

Higher and higher the cannonball flies
in a brilliant aerial burst
and catapulting through the skies
he lands in the net – feet first.

Jack Prelutsky

The Man on the Flying Trapeze

Sporting and capering high in the breeze,
cavorting about from trapeze to trapeze
is an aerial acrobat, slim as a ribbon,
as daring and free as a tree-swinging gibbon.

He hangs by his fingers, his toes and his knees,
he dangles and dips with astonishing ease,
then springs into space as though racing on wings,
gliding between his precarious swings.

He cheerfully executes perilous plunges,
dangerous dives, unforgettable lunges,
delicate scoops and spectacular swoops,
breathtaking triple flips, hazardous loops.

Then this midair magician with nerves made of steel
somersaults, catches and hangs by one heel.
As the audience roars for the king of trapezes
he takes out his handkerchief, waves it . . . and sneezes.

Balances above us, the high wire king
skips with a swivel, a sway and a swing.
He dances, he prances, he leaps through the air,
then hangs by his teeth while he's combing his hair.
He seems not to notice the perilous height
as he stands on his left hand and waves with his right.

Jack Prelutsky

Happiness

John had
Great Big
Waterproof
Boots on;
John had a
Great Big
Waterproof
Hat;

John had a
Great Big
Waterproof
Mackintosh –
And that
(Said John)
Is
That.

A. A. Milne

Where Have You Been?

Riding in the Rain

The rain comes pittering, pattering down,
  Plipperty, plipperty, plop!
The farmer drives his horse to town,
  Clipperty, clipperty, clop!
The rain comes pattering,
  The horse goes clattering,
    Clipperty, plipperty, plop!

Anon.

Sampan

Waves lap lap
Fish fins clap clap
Brown sails flap flap
Chop-sticks tap tap;

Up and down the long green river,
Oh hey, oh hey, lanterns quiver,
Willow branches brush the river,
Oh hey, oh hey, lanterns quiver.

Chop-sticks tap tap
Brown sails flap flap
Fish fins clap clap
Waves lap lap.

Anon.

Wagons, Trucks and Vans

This train is carrying passengers,
It's pulling ten coaches today
And when they get to Manchester
One coach will be taken away.

This train is carrying letters,
It's pulling nine mail vans today
And when they get to Birmingham
One van will be taken away.

This train is carrying coal dust,
It's pulling eight trucks today
And when they get to Canterbury
One truck will be taken away.

This train is carrying boxes,
It's pulling seven freight cars today
And when they get to Beverley
One car will be taken away.

This train is carrying people,
It's pulling six sleepers today
And when they get to Nottingham
One sleeper is taken away.

This train is carrying soldiers,
It's pulling five transports today
And when they get to Harrogate
One transport is taken away.

This train is carrying motor cars,
It's pulling four bogies today
And when they get to Leamington
One bogie is taken away.

This train is carrying parcels,
It's pulling three guard's vans today
And when they get to Inverness
One van will be taken away.

This train is carrying animals,
It's pulling two wagons today
And when they get to Scarborough
One truck will be taken away.

This train is carrying Her Majesty,
It's pulling the Royal Coach today
And when it gets to Edinburgh
THAT coach will be taken away.

Barbara Ireson

from Errantry

There was a merry passenger,
a messenger, a mariner:
he built a gilded gondola
to wander in, and had in her
a load of yellow oranges
and porridge for his provender;
he perfumed her with marjoram
and cardamom and lavender.

J. R. R. Tolkien

Hannibal

Hannibal crossed the Alps,
Hannibal crossed the Alps;
   With his black men,
   His brown men,
   His countrymen,
   His townmen,
With his Gauls and his Spaniards, his horses and elephants,
Hannibal crossed the Alps.

Hannibal crossed the Alps,
Hannibal crossed the Alps;
   For his bow-men,
   His spear-men,
   His front-men,
   His rear-men,
His Gauls and his Spaniards, his horses and elephants,
Wanted the Roman scalps!

And that's why
Hannibal, Hannibal, Hannibal,
Hannibal crossed the Alps.

Eleanor Farjeon

Anna Maria

Anna Maria she sat on the fire;
The fire was too hot, she sat on the pot;
The pot was too round, she sat on the ground;
The ground was too flat, she sat on the cat;
The cat ran away with Maria on her back.

Anon.

A Row of Red Coaches

A row of red coaches
Standing in a yard,
All summer long they've been
Working very hard:
Driving up the promenade,
Driving to the pier,
But now the visitors have gone
The quiet months are here.

Barbara Ireson

Down the Stream the Swans all Glide

Down the stream the swans all glide;
It's quite the cheapest way to ride.
Their legs get wet,
Their tummies wetter:
I think after all
The bus is better.

Spike Milligan

Skipping Song

The High Skip,
The Sly Skip,
The Skip like a Feather,
The Long Skip,
The Strong Skip,
And the Skip All Together!
The Slow Skip,
The Toe Skip,
The Skip Double-Double –
The Fast Skip,
The Last Skip,
And the Skip Against Trouble!

Anon.

The Blacksmith

A-hippity, hippity hop, heigh-ho!
Away to the blacksmith's shop we go.

If you've a pony
That's lost a shoe,
You can get her another
All shining and new –

A-hippity, hippity hop!

Anon.

I Visit the Queen

Ferdinand, Ferdinand,
Where have you been?
I've been up to London to look at the queen.
I've been with two horses,
A black and a grey;
They ate fifteen bundles
Of sweet-smelling hay.
At Buckingham Palace I stopped at the gate
And explained to the sentry why I was late.
The railings were splendid in black and in gold
And I tied up the horses and walked in the cold
Across the wide courtyard; the steps were so broad,
And someone in frockcoat said, 'Ticket, my Lord?'
I felt in my pocket – I knew it was there –
Mixed up with dog biscuits, and apple and pear.
And I bowed to the queen, and would you believe,
I remembered to cover the hole in my sleeve.
The queen very graciously chose not to see
The string round my trousers, the tear at my knee.
Ferdinand, Ferdinand,
What did you there?
I knelt to the queen and she touched my grey hair.

Gregory Harrison

Lightships

All night long when the wind is high
Nnn nnn nnnn
The lightships moan and moan to the sky
Nnn nnn nnnn.

Their foghorns whine when the mist runs free
Nnn nnn nnnn
Warning the men on the ships at sea
Nnn nnn nnnn.

Clive Sansom

Swim, Swan!

Swan swam over the sea,
   Swim, swan, swim!
Swan swam back again,
Well swum, swan!

Anon.

Little Billy Tailor

Little Billy Tailor
Gone to be a sailor,
His ship's for China bound;
Won't the sea perplex him!
Won't its rolling vex him!
I hope he won't get drowned.

Anon.

Me – Pirate

If ever I go to sea,
I think I'll be a pirate:
I'll have a treasure-ship in tow
And a man-of-war to fire at.

With a cutlass at my belt,
And a pistol in my hand,
I'll nail my Crossbones to the mast
And sail for a foreign land.

And when we reach that shore,
We'll beat our battle-drum
And fire a salute of fifteen guns
To tell them we have come.

We'll fight them all day long;
We'll seize their chests of gold,
Their diamonds, coins and necklaces,
And stuff them in our hold.

A year and a day at home,
Then off on the waves again –
Lord of the Caribbean Seas
King of the Spanish Main!

Clive Sansom

A Long Blue Dragon

The Shark

The shark
Swims
In the dark
Of the deep
Its eye gleams
As it sees
Streams
Of gold fish –
Bold fish
Swimming too near
For the shark is well aware
That here
Is a tasty dish
Of fish
And the shark lies
In wait –
No fisherman,
No flies
No bait.
And the fish swim past
The shark follows –
Fast,
And swallows.

Lalla Ward

The Dark Wood

In the dark, dark wood, there was
  a dark, dark house,
And in that dark, dark house, there was
  a dark, dark room,
And in that dark, dark room, there was
  a dark, dark cupboard,
And in that dark, dark cupboard, there was
  a dark, dark shelf,
And on that dark, dark shelf, there was
  a dark, dark box,
And in that dark, dark box, there was a
  GHOST!

Anon.

The Donkey

My mother bought a donkey – she thought it was a cow.
She sent me out to milk it, but I didn't know how.
The night was dark and I couldn't see,
And that old donkey took a bite out of me.

Anon.

Little Dick

Little Dick he was so quick,
He rushed to the window from his bed.
He bent his bow to shoot a crow
And shot the pussy-cat's tail instead.

Anon.

A Ham-bone and some Jellied Eels

A ham-bone and some jellied eels went knocking on a door,
They had just crept out of the grocery store,
The lady went upstairs to get a gun,
And you should have seen them jump and run.

Anon.

Twenty-five Robbers

Friday night at half past eight,
Twenty-five robbers came knocking on my gate.
I went out and let them in
And I hit each one with my rolling-pin.

Anon.

The Dreaded Tootsie-Kana

When the Tootsie-Kana comes,
Hide yourself behind your thumbs;
Tie a dustbin on your head;
Stay indoors; go to bed.

When the Tootsie-Kana goes,
Peel an apple with your toes;
Buy a sausage; paint it red –
Tootsie-Kana falls down dead.

Spike Milligan

The Hare

Between the valley and the hill
There sat a little hare;
It nibbled at the grass until
The ground was nearly bare.

And when the ground was nearly bare
It rested in the sun;
A hunter came and saw it there
And shot it with his gun.

It thought it must be dead, be dead,
But, wonderful to say,
It found it was alive instead
And quickly ran away.

Rose Fyleman

Have you seen the Hidebehind?

Have you seen the Hidebehind?
I don't think you will, mind you,
because as you're running through the dark
the Hidebehind's behind you.

Michael Rosen

Hog-pig waits on a mountain

Hog-pig waits on a mountain
  above a valley in the spring.
Hog-pig waits on a mountain
  above the valley where he is king.

He could – if he would
  chew up churches and trees
  ram his tusks through castle walls
  and bite through men-in-armour
  like a dog cracking fleas.

Hog-pig could trumpet in the air
  and make the valleys roar
or wait up on the mountain
  as he's always done before.

Michael Rosen

Heltery-Skeltery

Run, rabbit, run!
Run to your warren!
The harvest is done,
The meadow is barren.
The corn was your shelter
From stone, stick and gun,
Heltery, Skeltery,
Run, rabbit, run!

Eleanor Farjeon

A Monstrous Mouse

Just as I'd sucked in wind to take
A giant puff at my birthday cake,

While all the children sang and cheered,
Up shot the window shade – in peered

A monstrous mouse with jagged jaws!
Into the kitchen poked two paws

With fingernails like reindeer antlers!
The way a team of house-dismantlers

Bash houses down with a swinging ball,
He kicked – boom! – no more kitchen wall –

And through a new door to our kitchen
That wicked mouse, his whiskers twitchin',

Grabbed hold of my cake plate by both handles
And shouted, 'Yum! what nice hot candles!'

Straight through my cake his head went – squish!
I didn't have time to make a wish.

But when he pulled himself back out,
All fresh fruit frosting, his whole snout

Was fire! Sparks sputtered from each whisker!
You never did see mouse-dancing brisker.

Thick clouds of smoke choked our apartment.
My father phoned the Fire Department.

Up screeched four fire trucks, sirens roaring –
Nobody found *my* party boring!

Our bowl of orangeade and ice
Proved just the thing for dunking mice.

Mouse ran outside and down his tunnel
Faster than water through a funnel.

I sort of forget what games we played.
Nobody drank much orangeade.

                    X. J. Kennedy

The Ugstabuggle

Over by my bedroom wall
The ugstabuggle stands,
A monster nearly nine feet tall
With hairy, grasping hands.
In afternoons and mornings
He's always out of sight,
But often I can see him
In the darkness late at night.
Yet when I do not think of him
He disappears again,
And when I sleep he goes, because
I cannot see him then!

Peter Wesley-Smith

Green Man, Blue Man

As I was walking through Guildhall Square
I smiled to see a green man there,
But when I saw him coming near
My heart was filled with nameless fear.

As I was walking through Madford Lane
A blue man stood there in the rain.
I asked him in by my front-door,
For I'd seen a blue man before.

As I was walking through Landlake Wood
A grey man in the forest stood,
But when he turned and said, 'Good day'
I shook my head and ran away.

As I was walking by Church Stile
A purple man spoke there a while.
I spoke to him because, you see,
A purple man once lived by me.

But when the night falls dark and fell
How, O how, am I to tell,
Grey man, green man, purple, blue,
Which is which is which of you?

Charles Causley

A Thousand Hairy Savages

A thousand hairy savages
Sitting down to lunch
Gobble gobble glup glup
Munch munch munch

Spike Milligan

Bump

Things that go 'bump!' in the night,
Should not really give one a fright.
It's the hole in each ear
That lets in the fear,
That and the absence of light!

Spike Milligan

Creeping

A long blue dragon
  Is creeping through the village.
He's lashing his tail,
  And he's tossing his head.
Run, little children,
  Run into your houses;
Run into your houses,
  And jump into bed! . . .

Hilda Adams

Upstairs, downstairs

Upstairs, downstairs,
Creeping like a mouse,
Creeping in the darkness
Round and round the house.
Creep, creep, creeping,
Round and round about –
I hope the wind won't come inside
And blow my candle out.

Evelyn Abraham

The Three Mice

Three mice went into a hole to spin,
Puss passed by and she peeped in:
'What are you doing, my little men?'
'Weaving coats for gentlemen.'
'Please let me come in to wind off your thread.'
'Oh no, Mistress Pussy, you'll bite off our heads.'

Says Puss: 'You look so wondrous wise,
I like your whiskers and bright black eyes,
Your house is the nicest house I see,
I think there is room for you and me.'
The mice were so pleased that they opened the door,
And pussy soon laid them all dead on the floor.

Anon.

Oh, Who will Wash the Tiger's Ears?

Two Cats

When we opened the door late
to see what had happened to the sky
there were two cats
crouching among the snowdunes
pretending they were fireside laps.
The beads in their eyes stole some of
our kitchen light
and spilt it on to the path.
So we put down the bones of a chop there too
saying: there's some marrow inside that you know –
but they didn't believe it was for them
and sat still thawing their patches
like two warm loaves
and groaning that we hadn't put it near enough
seeing that they had put their feet to bed by now.

Michael Rosen

The Young Puppy

There was a young puppy called Howard,
Who at fighting was rather a coward;
    He never quite ran
    When the battle began,
But he started at once to bow-wow hard.

A. A. Milne

Higglety, pigglety, pop!

Higglety, pigglety, pop!
The dog has eaten the mop;
The pig's in a hurry,
The cat's in a flurry,
Higglety, pigglety, pop!

Anon.

Three Little Chickens

Said the first little chicken,
With a queer little squirm,
'Oh, I wish I could find
A fat little worm!'

Said the second little chicken,
With a little sigh of grief,
'Oh, I wish I could find
A little green leaf!'

Said the third little chicken,
With a sharp little squeal,
'Oh, I wish I could find
Some nice yellow meal!'

'Now, see here,' said their mother
From the green garden patch,
'If you want any breakfast,
You must all come and scratch!'

Anon.

I had a little moppet

I had a little moppet
And put it in my pocket
  And fed it on corn and hay.
There came a proud beggar
And swore he would have her,
  And stole my poor moppet away.
And through the wild wood she ran, ran, ran,
And through the wild wood she ran;
And all the long winter
She followed the hunter
  And never was heard of again.

Anon.

The Cow

The friendly cow all red and white,
  I love with all my heart;
She gives me cream with all her might,
  To eat with apple-tart.

She wanders lowing here and there,
  And yet she cannot stray,
All in the pleasant open air,
  The pleasant light of day;

And blown by all the winds that pass
  And wet with all the showers,
She walks among the meadow grass
  And eats the meadow flowers.

Robert Louis Stevenson

A Whale of a Tea-Time

Algernon Snail
Caught a very fine whale,
   And took it indoors for his tea;
But the end of this tale
Is the whale ate the snail –
   So the whale took the snail in for tea.

Carey Blyton

I went up the high hill

I went up the high hill,
There I saw a climbing goat;
I went down by the running rill,
There I saw a ragged sheep;
I went out to the roaring sea,
There I saw a tossing boat;
I went under the green tree,
There I saw two doves asleep.

Anon.

The Manatee

The sea-cow or grey manatee
Spends most of its time in the sea;
  But in tropical rainstorms
  It suffers from brainstorms
And hangs upside down in a tree.

Carey Blyton

My Animals

My animals are made of wool and glass,
Also of wood. Table and mantelpiece
Are thickly covered with them. It's because
You cannot keep real cats or dogs in these

High-up new flats. I really want to have
A huge, soft marmalade or, if not that,
Some animal that *seems* at least to love.
Hamsters? A dog? No, what I need's a cat.

I hate a word like 'pets'; it sounds so much
Like something with no living of its own.
And yet each time that I caress and touch
My wool or glass ones, I feel quite alone.

No kittens in our flat, no dogs to bark
Each time the bell rings. Everything is still;
Often I want a zoo, a whole Noah's ark.
Nothing is born here, nothing tries to kill.

Elizabeth Jennings

At the Zoo

First I saw the white bear, then I saw the black;
Then I saw the camel with a hump upon his back;
Then I saw the grey wolf, with mutton in his maw;
Then I saw the wombat waddle in the straw;
Then I saw the elephant a-waving of his trunk;
Then I saw the monkeys – mercy, how unpleasantly they – smelt!

William Makepeace Thackeray

The Elephant

The elephant carries a great big trunk;
He never packs it with clothes;
It has no lock and it has no key,
But he takes it wherever he goes.

Anon.

A Tomcat

Oh, the funniest thing I've ever seen
Was a tomcat sewing on a sewing machine.
Oh, the sewing machine got running too slow,
And it took seven stitches in the tomcat's toe.

Anon.

Drumming

Tum-tumpty-tum,
The cat is playing the drum;
Four little mice are shaking the ground,
Dancing merrily round and round,
Tum-tumpty-tum.

Tum-tumpty-tum,
The cat is playing the drum;
Three little mice are shaking the ground,
Dancing merrily round and round,
Tum-tumpty-tum.

Tum-tumpty-tum,
The cat is playing the drum;
Two little mice are shaking the ground,
Dancing merrily round and round,
Tum-tumpty-tum.

Tum-tumpty-tum,
The cat is playing the drum;
One little mouse is shaking the ground,
Dancing merrily round and round,
Tum-tumpty-tum.

Tum-tumpty-tum,
The cat is playing the drum;
No little mice are shaking the ground,
Dancing, dancing round and round,
Tum-tumpty-tum.

Anon.

from The Hedgehog

There's a hedgehog in the garden – come and see.
When he's still, he's like a pincushion that breathes.
When he moves, he's like a fat freckled mouse, following me
All over the place with pitter-patter feet.
He snorts and snuffs and sniffs my shoe,
Then hauls himself over the rise.

We'll introduce him to the cat. But she runs away
Into the box-tree, all hidden save her eyes
And nose and twitching tail –
Then suddenly leaps out and pounces.
(Can you blame her? He's drunk all
Her saucerful of milk, three fluid ounces.)

Caught?
Not likely. She pulls up short
And dances and prances and saws
The air all round him, mighty dainty with her paws;
Then, defeated, slinks away
To sulk or chase less prickly prey.

It's chilly now and getting late.
We'll cover him with a pile of autumn leaves
And let him hide or even hibernate.
In the morning we'll creep
Over the lawn and part the leaves and peer
Inside, and see if he's lying there asleep.
I hope he is . . .

He wasn't. He was out of his heap,
Waiting for me – wide awake perhaps all night? –
And came running towards me and round me and after me
All over the place with pitter-patter feet. . . .

Ian Serraillier

If I had a Donkey

If I had a donkey
That wouldn't go
D'you think I'd wallop him?
No! No! No!
I'd put him in a stable
And keep him nice and warm,
The best little donkey
That ever was born.
Gee up, Neddy,
Gee up, Neddy,
The best little donkey
That ever was born.

Anon.

The Caterpillar

Little Arabella Miller
Found a furry caterpillar,
And let it crawl upon her mother,
Then upon her baby brother;
Both cried, 'Naughty Arabella,
Take away the caterpillar.'

Anon.

Five Little Monkeys

Five little monkeys walked along the shore;
One went a-sailing,
Then there were four.
Four little monkeys climbed up a tree;
One of them tumbled down,
Then there were three.
Three little monkeys found a pot of glue;
One got stuck in it,
Then there were two.
Two little monkeys found a currant bun;
One ran away with it,
Then there was one.
One little monkey cried all afternoon,
So they put him in an aeroplane
And sent him to the moon.

Anon.

My Garden

Rabbits and moles
Always make holes.

It's a rabbit habit.

But the moles should be told
That my lawn is all-holed.

Barbara Ireson

Squirrel

The squirrel in the hickory tree's a
nervous fellow,
all quiver and scurry.
See him

hurl himself upon
a limb
worry a nut
pack his cheeks
race
downtree
to a secret place and
hurry
back
in furry frenzy.

There's something he knows
that makes him
go,
this soft slow
mellow
autumn day.

It has to do with
hunger
in the snow.

Lilian Moore

Dogs

The dogs I know
Have many shapes
For some are big and tall,
   And some are long,
      And
      some
      are thin,
And some are fat and small.
And some are little bits of fluff
And have no shape at all.

Marchette Chute

Cat

The black cat yawns,
Opens her jaws,
Stretches her legs,
And shows her claws.

Then she gets up
And stands on four
Long stiff legs
And yawns some more.

She shows her sharp teeth,
She stretches her lip,
Her slice of a tongue
Turns up at the tip.

Lifting herself
On her delicate toes,
She arches her back
As high as it goes.

She lets herself down
With particular care,
And pads away
With her tail in the air.

Mary B. Miller

Furry Bear

If I were a bear
   And a big bear too,
I shouldn't much care
   If it froze or snew;
I shouldn't much mind
   If it snowed or friz –
I'd be all fur-lined
   With a coat like his!

For I'd have fur boots and a brown fur wrap,
And brown fur knickers and a big fur cap.
I'd have a fur muffle-ruff to cover my jaws,
And brown fur mittens on my big brown paws.
With a big brown furry-down up to my head,
I'd sleep all winter in a big fur bed.

A. A. Milne

Oliphaunt

Grey as a mouse,
Big as a house,
Nose like a snake,
I make the earth shake,
As I tramp through the grass;
Trees crack as I pass.
With horns in my mouth
I walk in the South,
Flapping big ears.
Beyond count of years
I stump round and round,
Never lie on the ground,
Not even to die.
Oliphaunt am I,
Biggest of all,
Huge, old, and tall.
If ever you'd met me,
You wouldn't forget me.
If you never do,
You won't think I'm true;
But old Oliphaunt am I,
And I never lie.

J. R. R. Tolkien

Oh, Who will wash the Tiger's Ears?

Oh, who will wash the tiger's ears?
And who will comb his tail?
And who will brush his sharp white teeth?
And who will file his nails?

Oh, Bobby may wash the tiger's ears
And Susy may file his nails
And Lucy may brush his long white teeth
And I'll go down for the mail.

Shel Silverstein

I had a cow that gave rich milk

I had a cow that gave rich milk.
I made her a bonnet of dainty silk,
I fed her on the finest hay
And milked her twenty times a day.

Anon.

My Little Hen

I once had a little hen that never gave me eggs,
So I made her a coat and put stockings on her legs
And I gave her corn that I fetched from the store,
Then she laid ten big brown eggs just at my kitchen door.

Anon.

The Frog's Lament

'I can't bite
like a dog,'
said the bright
green frog.

'I can't dig,
I can't squirt,
I can't grip,
I can't hurt.

'All I can do
is hop and hide
when enemies come
from far and wide.

'I can't scratch
like a cat.
I'm no match
for a rat.

'I can't stab,
I can't snare,
I can't grab,
I can't scare.

'All I can do
my whole life through
is hop,' said the frog,
'and hide from view.'

And that's
what I saw him
up and do.

Aileen Fisher

The Mouse in the Wainscot

Hush, Suzanne!
Don't lift your cup.
That breath you heard
Is a mouse getting up.

As the mist that steams
From your milk as you sup,
So soft is the sound
Of a mouse getting up.

There! did you hear
His feet pitter-patter,
Lighter than tipping
Of beads in a platter,

And then like a shower
On the window pane
The little feet scampering
Back again?

O falling of feather!
O drift of a leaf!
The mouse in the wainscot
Is dropping asleep.

Ian Serraillier

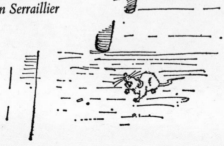

Bird Talk

Five little owls

Five little owls in an old elm-tree,
Fluffy and puffy as owls could be,
Blinking and winking with big round eyes
At the big round moon that hung in the skies:
As I passed beneath, I could hear one say,
'There'll be mouse for supper, there will, to-day!'
Then all of them hooted 'Tu-whit, Tu-whoo!
Yes, mouse for supper, Hoo hoo, Hoo hoo!'

Anon.

Pigeon and Wren

   Coo, coo, coo!
It's as much as a pigeon
   Can do
To bring up two!
But the little wren
   Can manage ten,
And bring them up
   Like gentlemen!

   Anon.

Green

Ducklings,
Look around.

That's treegreen
filling the sky

and there's grassgreen
running
up the hill
steeply.

The shadowgreen is
pine woods,
dark
old.

The yellowgreen is
young leaf
unfolding,
new
as you.

Breathe green
deeply.

Lilian Moore

Old Mother Minchin

Old Mother Minchin
When she was wed
Wanted to live
In a watercress bed.

Straw to sit on,
And reeds to press,
There she sat
In her Sunday dress!

What a peculiar
Thing to do!
But old Mother Minchin
Wasn't like you:

With a feather as strong
As a fine quill pen –
Old Mother Minchin,
My little moorhen!

Jean Kenward

Birds on a Stone

There were two birds
  Sat on a stone.
One flew away,
  Then there was one.
The other flew after,
  Then there was none,
And so the poor stone
Was left all alone.

        Anon.

Hen's Song

Chick, chick, come out of your shell,
I've warmed you long and I've warmed you well;
The sun is hot and the sky is blue
Quick, chick, it's time you came through.

        Rose Fyleman

Three Grey Geese

Three grey geese in a green field grazing:
In a green field grazing are three grey geese.
The grey geese graze while I am gazing:
I gaze and gaze till the grey geese cease.

        Anon.

Ducky-Daddles

Ducky-Daddles
Loves the puddles.
How he waddles
As he paddles
In the puddles –
Ducky Daddles!

W. Kingdon-Ward

The Merle and the Blackbird

The merle and the blackbird,
The laverock and the lark,
The plover and the lapwing –
How many birds is that?

Anon.

(Answer: three, because
merle and blackbird are the same
laverock and lark are the same
plover and lapwing are the same.)

The Last Word of a Bluebird
as Told to a Child

As I went out a Crow
In a low voice said, 'Oh,
I was looking for you.
How do you do?
I just came to tell you
To tell Lesley (will you?)
That her little Bluebird
Wanted me to bring word
That the north wind last night
That made the stars bright
And made ice on the trough
Almost made him cough
His tail feathers off.
He just had to fly!
But he sent her Good-bye,
And said to be good,
And wear her red hood,
And look for skunk tracks
In the snow with an axe –
And do everything!
And perhaps in the spring
He would come back and sing.'

Robert Frost

There was an old lady of France

There was an old lady of France
Who taught little ducklings to dance;
When she said, 'Tick-a-tack!' they only said 'Quack!'
Which grieved that old lady of France.

Edward Lear

I saw eight magpies in a tree

I saw eight magpies in a tree,
Two for you and six for me:

One for sorrow, two for mirth,
Three for a wedding, four for a birth,

Five for England, six for France,
Seven for a fiddler, eight for a dance.

Anon.

Quack

The duck is whiter than whey is,
His tail tips up over his back,
The eye in his head is as round as a button,
And he says, *Quack! Quack!*

He swims on his bright blue mill-pond,
By the willow-tree under the shack,
Then stands on his head to see down to the bottom,
And says, *Quack! Quack!*

When Molly steps out of the kitchen,
For apron – pinned round with a sack –
He squints at her round face, her dish, and what's in it,
And says, *Quack! Quack!*

He preens the pure snow of his feathers
In the sun by the wheat-straw stack;
At dusk waddles home with his brothers and sisters,
And says, *Quack! Quack!*

Walter de la Mare

Time to Rise

A birdie with a yellow bill
Hopped upon the window sill,
Cocked his shining eye and said:
'Ain't you 'shamed, you sleepy-head!'

Robert Louis Stevenson

Near and Far

What do hens say
With all their talking?
What luck! What luck! they cluck,
Look, look! they say
As they settle
In a sunny nook
And scoop
Dust under their feathers.

What does the ditch digging machine
Chatter about
Scratching
Into the dirt?
Who do I thank
For these scrumptious
Scrunchy
Chunks of rock? it asks
With a clatter and clank
As it stacks the cool earth up
In a neat brown bank.

Only in summer
The big machine
And loose old hens
Play the same scooping
Sunny game,
Saying the same things over and over
At about the same loudness
Because the machine is farther away.

Harry Behn

These Storks are Here to be Seen

There are storks
here you certainly
know it you hear them chatter
                    and bicker
                    and flutter
                    and jabber
                    and jostle
                    and babble
                    and cackle
                    and cuddle
                    and chortle
You build a sanctuary
and ask them to move, please.
Ask them to be a little quieter

if they will.

Carl Bagge

Eggs are laid by turkeys

Eggs are laid by turkeys
Eggs are laid by hens
Eggs are laid by robins
Eggs are laid by wrens
Eggs are laid by eagles
Eggs are laid by quail,
Pigeons, parrots, peregrines:
And that's how every bird begins.

Mary Ann Hoberman

Dead Blackbird

The blackbird used to come each day
listening, head-sideways, for movement under the lawn,
stabbing his yellow-as-crocus bill
precisely in,
pulling out a pink elastic worm.

In winter with flirted tail
he landed on the sill for crumbs
ousting sparrows, blue-tits – even robins.
Soot-black, sleek,
his plumage shone like a dark man's head.

Phoebe Hesketh

Bird Talk

'Think . . .' said the robin,
'Think . . .' said the jay,
sitting in the garden,
talking one day.

'Think about people –
the way they grow:
they don't have feathers
at all, you know.

They don't eat beetles,
they don't grow wings,
they don't like sitting
on wires and things.'
'Think!' said the robin.
'Think!' said the jay.
'Aren't people funny
to be that way?'

Aileen Fisher

The Swallows

Nine swallows sat on a telephone wire:
'Teeter, teeter,' and then they were still,
all facing one way, with the sun like a fire
along their blue shoulders, and hot on each bill.
But they sat there so quietly, all of the nine,
that I almost forgot they were swallows at all.
They seemed more like clothespins left out on the line
when the wash is just dried, and the first raindrops fall.

Elizabeth Coatsworth

In the Garden

Greedy little sparrow,
    Great big crow,
Saucy little tom-tits
    All in a row.

Are you very hungry,
    No place to go?
Come and eat my breadcrumbs,
    In the snow.

Anon.

That's the Way the Money Goes

Choosing Shoes

New shoes, new shoes,
Red and pink and blue shoes,
Tell me what would *you* choose
If they'd let us buy?

Buckle shoes, bow shoes,
Pretty pointy-toe shoes,
Strappy, cappy low shoes;
Let's have some to try.

Bright shoes, white shoes,
Dandy dance-by-night shoes,
Perhaps-a-little-tight shoes;
Like some? So would I.
BUT
Flat shoes, fat shoes,
Stump-along-like-that shoes,
Wipe-them-on-the-mat shoes
O that's the sort they'll buy.

Ffrida Wolfe

At the Super-market

Take a trolley,
  Push it round,
Castor sugar?
  Get a pound.
There's the cocoa,
  Take a tin.
Here's a loaf,
  But it's cut thin.
There's another.
  That will do.
Now we'll find
  Some jam for you.
Choose a jar.
  Yes, strawberry
Will suit your Dad
  And also me.
A tin of fish,
  A bag of rice,
That cream-filled cake
  Looks very nice.

We must have soap
    And toothpaste too,
This green shampoo
    Will do for you.
Apples and pears and
    Two pounds of peas,
A cabbage, a swede
    And a turnip, please.
I nearly forgot
    My jar of honey.
I wonder if we
    Have got enough money?
Push the trolley
    To the till.
I'll fetch a box
    For you to fill.
Leave the empty
    Trolley here.
My purse is empty
    Too, I fear.

Barbara Ireson

Coming from the Fair

Coming from the fair!
  Coming from the fair!
    We bought a little bottle
      For our baby over there;
        Alas, for we broke it,
          And we tried to buy another,
            But all the shops were closed,
              So we hurried home to mother.

Translated from a Chinese nursery rhyme *by I. T. Headland*

Gee up, Neddy

Gee up, Neddy, to the fair;
What shall we buy when we get there?
A penny apple and a penny pear;
Gee up, Neddy, to the fair.

Anon.

Banbury Fair

As I was going to Banbury,
  Upon a summer's day,
My dame had butter, eggs and fruit,
  And I had corn and hay.
Joe drove the ox, and Tom the swine,
  Dick took the foal and mare;
I sold them all – then home to dine,
  From famous Banbury Fair.

Anon.

Giddy Girls, Noisy Boys

Giddy girls, noisy boys,
  Come and buy my painted toys;
    Medals made of gingerbread,
      And penny horses white and red.

Anon.

Home From the Carnival

Gone all the lights and all the noise,
Gone all the cotton candy's joys,
And all my money spent and gone
With all the rides I rode upon
And all my money gone and spent
Upon the tables in the tent:
The Wheel of Fortune clicked and spun –
I lost my dimes and nothing won,
Not even from the bottom shelf.
I bring home nothing but myself,
And take to bed with meagre cheer
The teddy bear I won last year.

Russell Hoban

All for a Farthing

I went into my grandmother's garden,
And there I found a farthing.
I went into my next door neighbour's;
There I bought
A pipkin and a popkin,
A slipkin and a slopkin,
A nailboard, a sailboard,
And all for a farthing.

Anon.

Pop Goes the Weasel

Up and down the City Road,
  In and out the Eagle;
That's the way the money goes –
  Pop goes the weasel!

Half a pound of tuppenny rice,
  Half a pound of treacle;
Mix it up and make it nice –
  Pop goes the weasel!

Every night when I go out
  The monkey's on the table;
Take a stick and knock it off –
  Pop goes the weasel!

Anon.

If only I had plenty of money

If only I had plenty of money,
I'd buy you some flowers, and I'd buy you some honey,
I'd buy you a boat, and I'd buy you a sail,
I'd buy you a cat with a long bushy tail,
I'd buy you a brooch and a bangle as well,
I'd buy you a church, and I'd buy you the bell,
I'd buy you the earth, I'd buy you the moon –
Oh money, dear money, please come very soon.

Paul Edmonds

The Grocers

One grocer worked hard weighing rice,
Two grocers worked hard packing spice,
Three grocers worked hard sorting teas,
Four grocers worked hard wrapping cheese.
Five grocers worked hard stacking jam,
Six grocers worked hard slicing ham,
Seven grocers worked hard cutting meats,
Eight grocers worked hard opening sweets,
Nine grocers worked hard selling bread,
Ten grocers, tired out, went home to bed.

Barbara Ireson

The Friendly Cinnamon Bun

Shining in his stickiness and glistening with honey,
Safe among his sisters and his brothers on a tray,
With raisin eyes that looked at me as I put down my money,
There smiled a friendly cinnamon bun, and this I heard him say:

'It's a lovely, lovely morning, and the world's a lovely place;
I know it's going to be a lovely day.
I know we're going to be good friends; I like your honest face;
Together we might go a long, long way.'

The baker's girl rang up the sale, 'I'll wrap your bun,' said she.
'Oh no, you needn't bother,' I replied.
I smiled back at that cinnamon bun and ate him, one two three,
And walked out with his friendliness inside.

Russell Hoban

Come Christmas

Christmas Stocking

What will go into the Christmas Stocking
While the clock on the mantlepiece goes tick-tocking?
   An orange, a penny,
   Some sweets, not too many,
   A trumpet, a dolly,
   A sprig of red holly,
   A book and a top
   And a grocery shop,
   Some beads in a box,
   An ass and an ox
   And a lamb, plain and good,
   All whittled in wood,
   A white sugar dove,
   A handful of love,
   Another of fun,
   And it's very near done –
   A big silver star
   On top – there you are!
Come morning you'll wake to the clock's tick-tocking,
And that's what you'll find in the Christmas Stocking.

Eleanor Farjeon

The Pieman

As I was going down Mincing Lane,
Mincing Lane on a Christmas Day,
'Hot mince pies!' a pieman cries,
'Two for a penny, and look at the size!'

Anon.

On Christmas Day

There was a pig
  Went out to dig,
Christmas Day, Christmas Day,
  There was a pig
  Went out to dig
On Christmas Day in the morning.

There was a sow
  Went out to plough,
Christmas Day, Christmas Day,
  There was a sow
  Went out to plough
On Christmas Day in the morning.

There was a sparrow
  Went out to harrow,
Christmas Day, Christmas Day,
  There was a sparrow
  Went out to harrow
On Christmas Day in the morning.

There was a crow
  Went out to sow,
Christmas Day, Christmas Day,
  There was a crow
  Went out to sow
On Christmas Day in the morning.

There was a sheep
Went out to reap,
Christmas day, Christmas Day,
There was a sheep
Went out to reap
On Christmas Day in the morning.

Anon.

Christmas Pudding

Take milk, eggs, and raisins.
Take milk, eggs, and raisins; suet and
   sugar and flour.
Take milk, eggs, and raisins; suet and
   sugar and flour; candied-peel and breadcrumbs.
Take milk, eggs, and raisins; suet and
   sugar and flour; candied-peel and breadcrumbs -
   and boil for eight hours.

Anon.

It was a stormy night

It was a stormy night
One Christmas day
as they fell awake
on the Sante Fe

Turkey, jelly
and the ship's old cook
all jumped out
of a recipe book

The jelly wobbled
the turkey gobbled
and after them both
the old cook hobbled

Gobbler gobbled
Hobbler's Wobbler.
Hobbler gobbled
Wobbler's Gobbler.

Gobbly-gobbler
gobbled Wobbly
Hobbly-hobbler
Gobbled Gobbly.

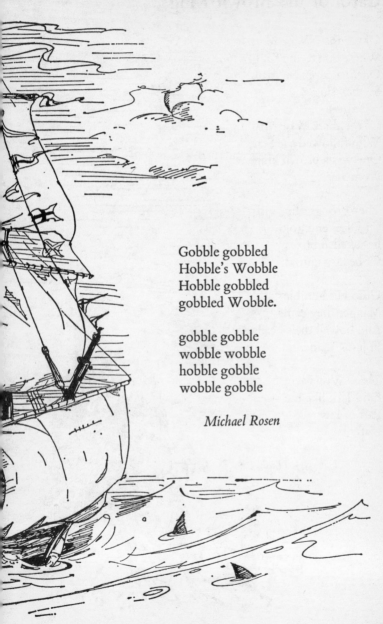

Gobble gobbled
Hobble's Wobble
Hobble gobbled
gobbled Wobble.

gobble gobble
wobble wobble
hobble gobble
wobble gobble

Michael Rosen

Carol of the Brown King

Of the three Wise Men
Who came to the King,
One was a brown man,
So they sing.

Of the three Wise Men
Who followed the Star,
One was a brown king
From afar.

They brought fine gifts
Of spices and gold
In jewelled boxes
Of beauty untold.

Unto His humble
Manger they came
And bowed their heads
In Jesus' name.

Three Wise Men,
One dark like me –
Part of His
Nativity.

Langston Hughes

Uncle John's Pig

When Uncle John brought home the pig on Christmas
   afternoon,
It didn't look like anything except a burst balloon,
A wiggly waggly pinky rag, as limp as limp could be;
'Call that a pig?' said little Jane: said Uncle, 'Wait and see.'

He blew into the pig and soon we saw it filling out;
He blew again and then we saw four legs, a little snout;
He blew once more, and then we saw the curly tail so neat,
He screwed it up and there it stood, the Perfect Pig complete.

A pig to join in any game so steady and so stout;
Then sometimes Uncle John, for fun would let the air run out,
And then we'd see it shrivel up and sink down dead – and then
Kind Uncle John would laugh and blow it back to life again.

But after Uncle John had gone (he went on Boxing Night),
Said Jane, 'Let's make it bigger now,' and soon she'd blown it
   tight;
She puffed and blew, and still it grew so big, so big, so BIG,
That with a mighty BANG . . . it burst . . . Oh, how I missed
   that pig!

Ffrida Wolfe

179

Advice to a child

Set your fir-tree
In a pot;
Needles green
Is all it's got.
Shut the door
And go away,
And so to sleep
Till Christmas Day.
In the morning
Seek your tree,
And you shall see
What you shall see.

Hang your stocking
By the fire,
Empty of
Your heart's desire;
Up the chimney
Say your say,
And so to sleep
Till Christmas Day.
In the morning
Draw the blind,
And you shall find
What you shall find.

Eleanor Farjeon

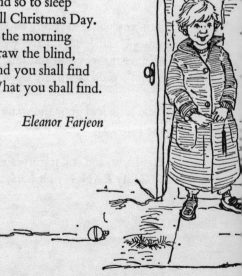

Little Tree

little tree
little silent Christmas tree
you are so little
you are more like a flower

who found you in the green forest
and were you very sorry to come away?
see i will comfort you
because you smell so sweetly

i will kiss your cool bark
and hug you safe and tight
just as your mother would,
only don't be afraid

look at the spangles
that sleep all the year in a dark box
dreaming of being taken out
                    and allowed to shine,
the balls the chains red
          and gold the fluffy threads,

put up your little arms
and i'll give them all to you to hold
every finger shall have its ring
and there won't be a single place
                    dark or   happy

then when you're quite dressed
you'll stand in the window
                for everyone to see
and how they'll stare!
oh but you'll be very proud

and my little sister and i will take hands
and looking up at our beautiful tree
we'll dance and sing
'Noel Noel'

e. e. cummings

In the Week When Christmas Comes

This is the week when Christmas comes.

Let every pudding burst with plums,
And every tree bear dolls and drums,
  In the week when Christmas comes.

Let every hall have boughs of green,
With berries glowing in between,
  In the week when Christmas comes.

Let every doorstep have a song
Sounding the dark street along,
  In the week when Christmas comes.

Let every steeple ring a bell
With a joyful tale to tell,
  In the week when Christmas comes.

Let every night put forth a star
To show us where the heavens are,
  In the week when Christmas comes.

Let every stable have a lamb
Sleeping warm beside its dam
  In the week when Christmas comes.

This is the week when Christmas comes.

Eleanor Farjeon

Index of first lines

Other great reads *from* **Red Fox**

Further Red Fox titles that you might enjoy reading are listed on the following pages. They are available in bookshops or they can be ordered directly from us.

If you would like to order books, please send this form and the money due to:

ARROW BOOKS, BOOKSERVICE BY POST, PO BOX 29, DOUGLAS, ISLE OF MAN, BRITISH ISLES. Please enclose a cheque or postal order made out to Arrow Books Ltd for the amount due, plus 22p per book for postage and packing, both for orders within the UK and for overseas orders.

NAME _____

ADDRESS _____

_____

Please print clearly.

Whilst every effort is made to keep prices low, it is sometimes necessary to increase cover prices at short notice. If you are ordering books by post, to save delay it is advisable to phone to confirm the correct price. The number to ring is THE SALES DEPARTMENT 071 (if outside London) 973 9700.

**Discover the exciting and hilarious books of
Hazel Townson!**

THE MOVING STATUE

One windy day in the middle of his paper round, Jason Riddle
is blown against the town's war memorial statue.

But the statue moves its foot! Can this be true?

ISBN 0 09 973370 6   £1.99

ONE GREEN BOTTLE

Tim Evans has invented a fantasic new board game called
REDUNDO. But after he leaves it at his local toy shop it
disappears! Could Mr Snyder, the wily toy shop owner have
stolen the game to develop it for himself? Tim and his friend
Doggo decide to take drastic action and with the help of a
mysterious green bottle, plan a Reign of Terror.

ISBN 0 09 956810 1   £1.50

THE SPECKLED PANIC

When Kip buys Venger's Speckled Truthpaste instead of
toothpaste, funny things start happening. But they get out of
control when the headmaster eats some by mistake. What terrible
truths will he tell the parents on speech day?

ISBN 0 09 935490 X   £1.75

THE CHOKING PERIL

In this sequel to *The Speckled Panic*, Herbie, Kip and Arthur
Venger the inventor attempt to reform Grumpton's litterbugs.

ISBN 0 09 950530 4   £1.25